Greek Takeout Recipes

Prepare Homemade Versions of Your
Favorite Greek Dishes
(2022 Cookbook for Beginners)

Sergios Konteas

TABLE OF CONTENTS

INTRODUCTION

Greek food is an amazing fusion of East and West. It is correct.

Mediterranean food at its finest, with a wide range of influences. According to the

The touches of exotic spices come from the East, while the touches of leather come from the West.

Garlic and tomato are traditional Italian ingredients. Greek cuisine makes use of fresh food and what is plentiful in various locations of Greece .Cereals, legumes, veggies, meat, fish, olive oil, and so on rice. Wine is often served during meals. Greek cuisine is not only delicious but also healthy.

It's excellent, with its distinct color and taste combinations.

Employing low-fat, high-nutritional-value components To appreciate Greek cuisine, To relish gastronomy is to taste history, culture, and love. Every Greek housewife cooks deliberately crafts recipes using the freshest ingredients seasoned with herbs and spices — cooked according to an age-old custom nutrition preservation for a happy and healthy family

HISTORY

Takeaway cuisine has been a part of Greek culture since ancient times, going back to the days of Pompeii, yet Greek takeout in America has evolved through time to accommodate the North American palette.

Depending on availability, American components have been added.

In the United States, for example, Greek salad incorporates lettuce, which is not featured in the original recipe. Traditional Greek cuisine of legumes and greens has been supplanted with new concoctions comprising more meat and dairy.

Many renowned Greek foods, such as moussaka and tzatziki, were invented in the early 1900s and are truly Arabic in origin. Tomatoes are claimed to have first appeared in Greek cuisine in the 1920s. Moreover, although traditional Greek recipes use basic cooking procedures, many foods presently use French culinary techniques.

Greek chef Nicholas Tselementes, who published his cookbook in the 1920s, had a significant effect on modern Greek cookery.

Elements used numerous French methods and made an attempt to create what he thought were authentically authentic Greek dishes. His handbook became the bible for many Greek chefs, and his recipes are regarded to be the foundation of contemporary Greek food.

Greek yogurt surged in popularity in the late 1990s after becoming popular in the late 1980s. This is attributed to the (misguided) belief that everything Mediterranean is low in fat and hence healthy. True Greek yogurt is supposed to have a high-fat content. What is marketed as "Greek" yogurt in the United States may really be Bulgarian or Turkish.

Because of the fresh, uncomplicated, and low-fat ingredients, Greek and other Mediterranean recipes have been popular since the early 1990s.

Olive oil was shown to be superior to maize, soybean, and butter oils. Mediterranean food is known as a healthful diet as a result of its emphasis on fish and fresh ingredients.

Greek cuisine is unquestionably tasty. When you cook at home, you have a say in selecting fresh, healthy foods as well as cooking techniques. You can get the joy of saving money on large takeaway dinners and customizing the recipes to your own tastes.

Ingredients

Traditionally, this traditional meal uses the most basic and simple ingredients, such as grains, olive oil, and wine. Here is a list of some of the items you can come across in Greek cookery.

Dairy

The Mediterranean environment promoted the growth of sheep and goats over cattle, as well as the preservation of milk by curdling - the production of cheese and yogurt. There are various varieties of Greek cheeses, the most well-known of which is Feta. Greek yogurt is produced by straining out the whey, resulting in a thicker, higher protein-content product.

Shellfish and fish

Because Greece is surrounded by water, fish such as tuna, mullet, sardines, bass, and anchovies are regularly utilized.

Fruits are often seen in Greek meals rather than expensive sweets provided on special occasions. Fruits such as grapes, apples, pears, and figs are commonly found in Greek meals. They may be both fresh and dried.

Grains

Wheat and barley are the most common grains in Greek cuisine, and they are often used to produce bread and pasta. Rice is also used to make pilafs and dolmades (wrapped in grape leaves).

Spices and herbs

Flat-leaf parsley, dill, oregano, cilantro, thyme, mint, cumin, cinnamon, and scarlet saffron are all popular herbs. The majority of the time, dried herbs are utilized, and they are also recognized for their medicinal effects.

7

Pepper should be ground fresh.

Legumes

Chickpeas, lima beans, split peas, and lentils are used in a variety of dishes including stews, bakes, pilafs, soups, and salads. They may be pureed and used to create dips.

Meat is utilized less commonly in traditional Greek cuisine than in takeaway recipes. Meats are traditionally reserved for exceptional occasions.

Beef and pig are the most common meat sources, while sheep and goats are utilized for milk.

Greeks like nuts including pine nuts, almonds, walnuts, and pistachios.

Olives are a Greek staple that has been grown for millennia.

The most popular olives are brownish-black Kalamata olives, which are used in appetizers, stews, and salads.

Extra virgin olive oil

Olive oil has been used since ancient times, and Greek olive oil is considered to be among the finest in the world. It's often produced using the Koroneiki olive. Extra virgin olive oil (EVOO) is the most often used kind in Greek cookery. It is the first product of cold pressing the olive fruit and is the primary fat in Greek cookery. It may also be used as a salad dressing or dip.

Poultry Chicken, quail, and guinea fowl are common ingredients in traditional Greek cooking.

Vegetables

Vegetables have always been an important feature of Greek cuisine.

Zucchini, eggplant, spinach, artichokes, and tomatoes are popular veggies.

Wine

Wine is another important component of Greek cuisine, albeit it is only drunk in moderation and accompanying meals. Greek wine comes in red, white, sweet, and dry varieties. The most common alcoholic beverage in Greece is ouzo, an anise-flavored liqueur.

Yogurt

Greek yogurt has a thicker consistency than most other forms of yogurt. It has been depleted of whey, making it higher in protein and lower in carbs. Traditional versions are prepared from goat's and sheep's milk, while current ones are created from cow's milk. Yogurt is used in Greek cookery as a béchamel sauce for baked meats or as a sour element. It may also be used as a breakfast condiment, dip, or toast spread.

Methods of Cooking

Greek food employs conventional techniques such as boiling, stewing, broiling or grilling, sautéing, baking, and frying.

When greens are in season, they are frequently cooked. Oil, primarily olive oil, is used in varying quantities for sautéing, frying, or as an ingredient in stews, salads, and just about anything. With olive oil and tomatoes, many meat recipes are stewed or slow-cooked. Olive oil is used to fry or sauté meatballs, zucchini, potatoes, pumpkin, and even cheese.

In Greek cookery, shallow pans or clay pots are used to bake a range of meals including lamb, fish, potatoes, tomatoes, and other vegetables, as well as desserts. Meats are either cooked over charcoal or roasted.

Cooking Supplies

Anyone with a well-equipped kitchen and basic culinary gear and equipment can make Greek meals. Here are some more useful additions.

Processor of Food

This is a helpful tool in any cuisine. Greek recipes abound with dips and sauces that need the preparation of purees and pastes.

Graters Greek cookery makes use of entire spices that are grated just before use, which results in a more flavorful dish. Small graters are useful for adding just the perfect quantity of spices or cheese to a dish while cooking.

Baking pans and tins made of metal

These are required for baking veggies, pies, or pastries.

Pestle and Mortar

In a mortar and pestle, crush, pound, and grind fresh herbs, spices, and some vegetables. It's a great tool for Greek cookery.

Can Olive Oil Be Used?

11

Olive oil is often used in Greek cookery. Small amounts of olive oil may be easily poured from the can.

Brush for Pastry

This method is often used to coat doughs, vegetables, meat, or baking items with oil, butter, or glazes.

Grinder for pepper

This is particularly useful since Greek cookery calls for freshly ground pepper.

Saucepans come in a variety of sizes. Cooking many ingredients separately and all at once on the stovetop is common in Greek recipes.

Souvlaki skewers made of steel

Steel is superior to wood since it is reusable and more durable.

Rolling Pin Made of Straight Wood

When preparing Greek bread, you may use one to create uniform pressure.

Whisks

For recipes that call for lemon oil, béchamel sauce, or egg combinations.

Spatulas and wooden spoons

Have a variety of shapes and sizes on hand. Useful for mixing, ladling, tossing, spreading, smoothing, and other similar tasks.

The recipes on this page will allow you to recreate your favorite Greek takeaway dishes in the comfort of your own home. Let's get started now that you've gathered your supplies and tools.

Appetizers

Keftedakia is a Greek meatball dish.

4 servings

Time to Prepare: 10 minutes

Time to cook: 20 minutes

Ingredients

2 slices of white bread, 1 inch thick

½ cup milk

3 tablespoons extra-virgin olive oil (EVOO)

1 ½ pounds ground lamb or beef

Freshly ground pepper

Kosher salt

¼ cup fresh mint, finely chopped

3 tablespoons red onion, grated

1 tablespoon fresh oregano, finely chopped

¼ teaspoon ground cinnamon

2 cloves garlic, grated or crushed to a paste

1 large egg

Juice of ½ a lemon

4 pocket-less pitas or flatbreads, cut into wedges

Tzatziki

Meatballs with pita bread instructions

1. Preheat the oven to 450 degrees Fahrenheit.

2. Set a cooling rack on top of a baking sheet or metal pan.

3. Soak the bread pieces in the milk for a few minutes.

4. Combine the EVOO, meat, and pepper in a mixing dish. Season with salt and pepper.

5. Combine the mint, onions, oregano, cinnamon, smashed garlic, egg, and lemon juice in a mixing bowl.

6. Squeeze extra milk off the bread and cut it into pieces. Combine it with the meat mixture.

7. Using your hands or an ice cream scoop, shape the meat mixture into balls.

8. Place the meatballs on a cooling rack over a baking sheet and bake for approximately 15 minutes, or until cooked through.

15

9. Grill the pita bread until it is gently toasted and has some dark streaks (about 1 minute on each side).

10. Toss the meatballs with the grilled pita bread and tzatziki.

Dolmades are grape leaves that have been stuffed.

6 people

Time to Prepare: 30 minutes

1 hour 10 minutes to cook

Ingredients

1 8-ounce jar of grape leaves, rinsed and drained

¼ cup extra-virgin olive oil (EVOO)

1 cup chicken stock

Juice of 2 lemons

For the filling

¼ cup extra-virgin olive oil (EVOO)

1 large yellow onion, finely chopped

1 small fennel bulb, halved, cored, and diced

1 teaspoon lemon zest, grated

½ cup pine nuts

1 cup long-grain rice

½ cup chicken stock

2 tablespoons dill leaves, finely chopped

¼ cup flat-leaf parsley, finely chopped

Kosher salt

Freshly ground black pepper

Instructions for Filling

1. Heat the oil in a large saucepan over medium heat.

2. Stir in the onion, fennel, and lemon zest until tender (approximately 10 minutes).

3. Combine the pine nuts and rice in a mixing bowl (about 2 minutes).

4. Pour in the chicken stock.

5. Reduce the heat to low and continue to cook until the rice is al dente (approximately 10 minutes).

6. Place the rice mixture in a mixing bowl and toss in the remaining filling ingredients.

7. Remove from the oven and set aside to cool.

How to Make Grape Leaves

8. Blanch the grape leaves for 5 minutes in boiling water until malleable.

Drain.

18

9. Remove the leaves' stems and stiff veins.

10. Using paper towels, pat dry.

to put together/wrap

11. Place a grape leaf, glossy side down, on a flat surface.

12. Place 2 tablespoons of the rice filling at the stem end of the leaf.

13. Fold the stem end over the filling, then fold both sides toward the center, rolling up securely like a cigar, but leaving a little room or looseness for rice to expand.

14. Squeeze the roll softly to secure it.

15. Continue until there are no more leaves or filling left.

Preparing the dolmades

16. Arrange the dolmades in a single layer, seam side down, in a large saucepan or Dutch oven.

17. Drizzle the dolmades with olive oil, broth, and lemon juice. If necessary, add water until the liquid reaches halfway up the rolls.

18. Cover and cook for 30 to 40 minutes on low heat.

When probed with a fork, dolmades should be delicate.
19

Spinach Pie Spanakopita

Serves 8

Preparation Time: 15 minutes, plus overnight thawing

Time to cook: 45 minutes

Ingredients

1 8-ounce sheet puff pastry, thawed in the refrigerator overnight

2 tablespoons flour for dusting, or as needed

20

1 large egg, optional

For filling

1 tablespoon olive oil

1 small yellow onion, diced

1 clove of garlic, minced

1 cup cottage cheese

¼ cup Parmesan cheese

2 large eggs

½ teaspoon salt

Freshly ground pepper

⅛ teaspoon ground nutmeg

2 cups frozen cut spinach, thawed in the refrigerator overnight

Instructions for Filling

1. Preheat the oven to 375 degrees Fahrenheit.

2. Saute the onion and garlic in olive oil in a pan over medium heat until tender (about 5 minutes).

21

3. In the meanwhile, thoroughly combine the cheeses, eggs, salt, pepper, and nutmeg in a mixing bowl.

4. Place the thawed spinach in a sieve or strainer and squeeze out as much liquid as you can. Combine it with the cheese mixture.

5. Add the softened garlic and onion that have been sautéed. Combine thoroughly.

Spread the puff pastry out on a floured work surface and roll into a 12-inch by 12-inch square.

7. Line a 9-inch pie pan with the rolled dough.

8. Fill the pastry-lined pan equally with the filling for baking

9. Fold the pastry corners back over the top of the filling.

10. Brush the top with a whisked egg (optional).

11 Cook for 45 minutes at 350°F.

12 Set aside for 5 minutes before slicing.

Tiropita - Cheese-Stuffed Puff Pastry

9 people

1 hour and 10 minutes to prepare

Time to cook: 20 minutes

Ingredients

1 sheet puff pastry (8 ounces) Flour for dusting

1 big beaten egg

2 cups crumbled feta cheese

2 tbsp poppy seeds or sesame seeds (optional)

1 big beaten egg for glazing

Directions

1. Prepare a baking sheet by lining it with parchment paper and setting it aside.

2. In a mixing dish, combine the beaten egg and crumbled feta.

3. On a floured surface or cutting board, cut the puff pastry into 9 squares.

4. Spread one-half of the square with a heaping spoonful of feta filling. Allow roughly a 1/2-inch leeway around the edges of the dough for sealing.

5. Fold the dough in half to form a triangle and press the corners together to seal. Place it on a baking sheet that has been lined with parchment paper.

6. Continue until all of the squares are filled.

7. Refrigerate until solid (approximately 1 hour) or freeze for later use.

Preheat the oven to 425 degrees Fahrenheit.

9. Brush the tops of the pies with beaten egg and, if preferred, sprinkle with poppy or sesame seeds.

10. Bake until golden brown (about 15 minutes or less). Do not defrost if frozen before baking.

11. Keeps for two days at room temperature.

Fries with Feta

6-8 people

Time to Prepare: 5 minutes

Time to cook: 15-30 minutes

Ingredients

1 32-ounce bag of french fries

Oil for frying

½ tablespoon oregano

1 teaspoon parsley

1 teaspoon thyme

⅓ cup feta, crumbled

Kosher salt, to taste

Freshly ground pepper

Directions

1. In a mixing basin, combine the oregano, parsley, thyme, and feta.

Season with salt (but not too much) and pepper to taste.

2. Cook the french fries according to package directions.

Using paper towels, drain. (Alternatively, brush them with olive oil and bake them at 400°F for 30 minutes, turning once after 20 minutes.)

3. Garnish with feta mixture and serve.

Fritters with Zucchini

6 to 12 people

Time to prepare: 5 minutes + 10 minutes standing time

Time to cook: 15-30 minutes

Ingredients

2 medium zucchini, trimmed and shredded

1 teaspoon salt

2 scallions, minced

27

2 tablespoons fresh dill, minced

½ cup feta cheese, crumbled

1 clove of garlic, minced or pressed through a garlic press

¼ teaspoon black pepper

¼ cup cornstarch

½ teaspoon baking powder

6 tablespoons olive oil, divided

2 large eggs, beaten

Lemon wedges, for serving

Directions

1. Season the shredded zucchini with salt and place it in a colander over a basin. Allow it to rest for 10 minutes before pressing down or squeezing with your hands to remove any extra liquid.

2. Combine the zucchini, scallions, dill, feta, garlic, and black pepper in a large mixing basin.

3. Sift the cornstarch and baking powder over the mixture and well combine.

4. Heat 3 tablespoons of olive oil in a nonstick pan over medium heat.

5. Spoon 2 teaspoons of the zucchini mixture onto the pan, spreading it out into a circle and pushing down to form 2-inch-wide fritters.

6. Cook for about 2-3 minutes on each side. Using paper towels, drain.

7. Add the remaining oil and cook the remaining zucchini mixture into fritters.

8. Garnish with lemon wedges.

Fried calamari

4-8 servings

Time to Prepare: 10 minutes

Time to cook: 15 minutes

Ingredients

25 ounces calamari, cleaned, washed, and drained
30

1 tablespoon freshly ground pepper

2 tablespoons salt

½ tablespoon paprika

1 tablespoon oregano

¾ cup bread flour

½ cup semolina flour

Oil for frying

Lemon wedges

Directions

1. Slice the calamari into 1/2-inch rings and drain on paper towels, but do not pat dry.

2. Using a mortar and pestle, food processor, or blender, grind the spices into a powder.

3. In a resealable bag or plastic container, combine the spices and flour.

4. Toss the calamari rings in the flour mixture to coat.

5. Gently brush off any excess flour after removing the rings from the flour mixture. Place them on a platter.

6. In a deep pan or fryer, heat 2 to 3 inches of oil.

7. When the oil starts to bubble, test it with a single ring. The calamari should begin to sizzle. This indicates that the oil is at the proper temperature.

8. Fry the calamari in batches (not too many at a time for crispier results) for approximately 2-3 minutes, or until golden brown.

9. Drain on paper towels after removing from the oil using a sieve or slotted spoon.

10. Garnish with freshly squeezed lemon.

Fried Cheese Saganaki

6 people

Time to Prepare: 5 minutes

Time to cook: 10 minutes

Ingredients

1 pound krinos kefalograviera, kasseri or graviera cheese, cut into 2-

inch by ½-inch pieces

Flour (for dredging)

½ cup olive oil

2 lemons, cut into wedges

1 pinch dry Oregano

Grilled or toasted pita bread (optional)

Directions

1. Rinse and coat each piece of sliced cheese with flour after rinsing it under cold tap water.

2. In a pan, heat the oil and brown the cheese on both sides.

33

3. Drain on paper towels before serving with lemon wedges and a pinch of oregano. If preferred, serve with grilled or toasted pita.

SALADS

Salad with Marouli

serves 6 people.

Time to Prepare: 10 minutes

Time to cook: 0 minutes

Ingredients:

1 romaine lettuce head

4 sliced onions 3 tablespoons chopped fresh dill Olive oil

Vinegar of white wine

1 lemon's salt juice (optional)

Directions

1. Clean the lettuce by thoroughly washing the leaves in cold water. Drain thoroughly.

2. Finely chop the lettuce.

3. In a mixing bowl, combine the lettuce, scallions, and dill.

4. To taste, add the lemon juice (optional), salt, olive oil, and vinegar.

Tomato Greek Salad

serves 6 people.

35

Time to prepare: 2 hours marinating time (or less)

Time to cook: 0 minutes

Ingredients

4 fresh tomatoes, chopped

1 cucumber, peeled and chopped

1 green bell pepper, cut into ½-inch pieces

½ cup red onion, chopped

¼ cup Kalamata olives

½ cup feta cheese, crumbled

For the dressing

1 tablespoon red wine vinegar

1 tablespoon balsamic vinegar

1 tablespoon extra-virgin olive oil

1 teaspoon salt

1 tablespoon fresh oregano, chopped

Directions

1. Combine the dressing ingredients in a mixing bowl.

2. Toss in the remaining ingredients.

3. Refrigerate for 2 hours (or less) to let flavors mingle.

4. Plate and serve.

Salad Santorini

serves 2 people.

Time to Prepare: 5 minutes
37

Time to cook: 0 minutes

Ingredients

½ cucumber, peeled, halved, and sliced

½ red onion, thinly sliced

¾ green bell pepper, thinly sliced

½ cup Greek olives

½ cup cherry tomatoes halved

2 teaspoons olive oil

1 teaspoon oregano

1 tablespoon dill, chopped

Salt and pepper

1 slice of feta cheese

1 tablespoon capers

Directions

1. In a mixing bowl, combine all of the ingredients EXCEPT the feta and capers.

2. Arrange the feta cheese on top and garnish with capers before serving.

Salad Santorini

serves 2 people.

Time to Prepare: 5 minutes

Time to cook: 0 minutes

Ingredients

½ cucumber, peeled, halved, and sliced

½ red onion, thinly sliced

¾ green bell pepper, thinly sliced

½ cup Greek olives

½ cup cherry tomatoes halved

2 teaspoons olive oil

1 teaspoon oregano

1 tablespoon dill, chopped

Salt and pepper

1 slice of feta cheese

1 tablespoon capers

Directions

1. In a mixing bowl, combine all of the ingredients EXCEPT the feta and capers.

2. Arrange the feta cheese on top and garnish with capers before serving.

Salad with Eggplant (Melitzanosalata)

Preparation Time: 20 minutes

Serves: 1-2

1 hour of cooking time

Ingredients

3 eggplants, washed and pierced all over with a fork

2 cloves garlic, crushed

Parsley sprigs, finely chopped

Salt

Ground black pepper

3 tablespoons olive oil

2 tablespoons red wine vinegar, or according to taste

½ cup feta cheese

Directions

1. Preheat the oven to 350 degrees Fahrenheit.

2. Bake the perforated eggplants for 1 hour at 350°F. The eggplant should be tender, with a little burned skin.

3. Peel and finely cut the eggplants.

4. In a mixing dish, combine the eggplants, garlic, parsley, salt, and pepper.

5. Stir in the olive oil gradually, followed by vinegar.

6. The eggplants should be almost soft but still somewhat chunky.

7. Fold in the feta crumbles.

Salad à la grecque

6 people

Time to prepare: 20 minutes + 30 minutes sitting time

Time to cook: 0 minutes

Ingredients

1 cucumber, unpeeled, seeded, and sliced ¼-inch thick

1 red bell pepper, diced

1 yellow bell pepper, diced

1 cup cherry tomatoes, halved

½ red onion, sliced in half-rounds

8 ounces feta cheese, ½-inch diced

½ cup Kalamata olives pitted

For vinaigrette

2 cloves garlic, minced

1 teaspoon dried oregano
43

½ teaspoon Dijon mustard

¼ cup red wine vinegar

1 teaspoon kosher salt

½ teaspoon freshly ground black pepper

½ cup olive oil

Directions

1. In a small mixing bowl, combine all of the vinaigrette ingredients EXCEPT the olive oil.

2. Slowly drizzle in the olive oil, whisking constantly, to create an emulsion. Set it aside for now.

3. In a large mixing basin, combine the cucumber, peppers, tomatoes, and red onion.

4. Drizzle the vinaigrette over the veggies and mix with the feta and olives to combine.

5. Enable it to rest for 30 minutes, unrefrigerated, to allow the flavors to mingle.

Salad Kolonaki - Greek Salad with Roasted Chicken

6 people

Time to prepare: 20 minutes + 30 minutes to 4 hours marinating

Time to cook: 10 minutes

1 recipe Greek Salad Ingredients

4 fillets of chicken breast

For the marinade

1 lemon, freshly squeezed

2 tbsp olive oil (extra-virgin)

1 tsp. dried oregano

season with salt to taste

10 tsp black pepper

Directions

45

1. Make the marinade for the chicken by combining all of the marinade ingredients in a plastic, glass, stainless steel, or another non-reactive dish.

2. Coat the chicken fillets with the marinade and massage them in.

3. Wrap with plastic wrap and place in the refrigerator.

4. Marinate in the refrigerator for 30 minutes to 4 hours.

5. Prepare and put away the Greek salad.

6. Once the chicken is done, heat a nonstick or heavy-bottomed pan over high heat.

7. Cook the chicken for around 4-5 minutes before flipping it over to cook the other side for another 4-5 minutes. Check to see whether it is completely cooked.

8. Place the chicken on a chopping board and set it aside for 5 minutes to rest.

9. Cut it into small strips and lay them on top of the Greek salad.

ten. Serve

SOUPS

Soup Avgolemono (Lemon-Chicken-Rice)

Serves: 4-6 people

Time to Prepare: 15 minutes

Time to cook: 20 minutes

Ingredients

6 cups chicken broth

1 teaspoon fresh dill, finely chopped

47

½ cup uncooked orzo or rice-shaped pasta

4 large eggs

⅓ cup fresh lemon juice

1 large carrot, peeled and shredded

¼ teaspoon salt

¼ teaspoon white pepper

8 ounces chicken breast fillet, cut into bite-sized pieces

Directions

1. Combine the chicken broth and dill in a large pot.

2. Bring the water to a boil. Reduce the heat to low and add the orzo.

3. Cook for 5 minutes, or until the orzo is just soft.

Take the pan off the heat.

4. In a blender, combine the eggs and lemon juice and pulse until smooth.

5. While the blender is running, gently pour in the majority of the broth (make sure there is no orzo). Set aside after blending until smooth.

6. Meanwhile, combine the remaining broth-orzo combination with the carrot, salt, pepper, and chicken.

7. Bring it to a low boil over medium heat.

8. Cook until the chicken and orzo are tender (about 5 minutes).

9. Reduce the heat to low and gradually whisk in the egg mixture from the blender.

Cook for another 30 seconds, stirring regularly.

11. Serve right away.

Tomato Soup (Domatosoupa)

servings 4

Time to prepare: 20 minutes

1 hour of cooking time

Ingredients

3 sundried tomatoes, snipped
50

½ cup boiling water

1 large sweet onion, peeled and finely chopped

1 medium leek, washed and finely chopped, whites only

3 tablespoons olive oil

1 4 ½-ounce can diced tomatoes, with the juice

1 teaspoon sugar

1 garlic clove, minced

Zest of ½ an orange, grated

2 tablespoons fresh mint, finely chopped

4 ½ cups herb broth (store-bought or homemade) or vegetable broth

1 ½ cups Greek yogurt

1 tablespoon all-purpose flour

Salt and freshly ground black pepper, to taste

½ cup flat-leaf parsley, minced

Directions

51

1. Soak the sundried tomatoes in boiling water for 10 minutes to soften. Remove the water.

2. In a mortar and pestle, pound the sundried tomatoes with their juice until a paste forms.

3. Saute the onion and leek in olive oil in a heavy-bottomed saucepan until transparent.

4. Combine the chopped tomatoes, sundried tomato paste, and sugar in a mixing bowl.

5. Cook for 2-3 minutes over medium-high heat.

6. Cook for 3 minutes more after adding the garlic, orange zest, and mint.

7. Gradually add the herb or vegetable broth, cover, and continue to cook for another 30-45 minutes.

8. In a mixing basin, combine the yogurt and flour until smooth.

9. Add a tablespoon of hot soup at a time, stirring frequently.

10. Continue to stir while adding another tablespoon of soup.

11. Stir frequently as you slowly add the yogurt mixture to the soup pot.

12. Cook the soup over low heat, stirring regularly.

There should be no curdling of the milk.

13. Taste and adjust the spices as desired.

14. Garnish with parsley and serve immediately.

Sandwiches/Wraps

Greek Pita Bread

serves 8-16 people.

Time to prepare: 25 minutes + 1 hour for proofreading

Time to cook: 20 minutes
53

Ingredients

4 cups all-purpose flour + more, if needed

2 teaspoons fresh thyme, chopped (optional)

1 tablespoon olive oil + more for brushing

For yeast

1 envelope (7 g or 2 ¼ teaspoons) dry yeast

1 tablespoon sugar

½ cup warm (not hot) water

For salt

1 cup of warm water

2 teaspoons salt

Directions

1. Combine the yeast, sugar, and warm water in a small mixing basin.

Allow for a 10-minute resting period. The presence of froth on the surface shows that the yeast has been active.

2. Dissolve the salt in the water in a separate small basin or cup.

3. Combine the flour and thyme, if used, in a third large mixing basin. Fill a big well in the middle with the yeast mixture.

4. Before adding the salt and water solution, mix in roughly 3 strokes with a wooden spoon or the hook attachment of your mixer.

5. Mix for a minute or two, or until everything is well incorporated. If the dough is too sticky, gently add additional flour, or gradually add water if it is too dry.

6. Knead the dough until it is smooth (about 15 minutes). When pinched, the dough should withdraw.

7. Knead the oil into the dough gradually until it is fully integrated.

8. Brush the dough with oil and set it in a clean, dry basin.

9. Brush the dough's surface with a little additional oil and cover the bowl with a cloth or aluminum foil.

10. Set it aside in a warm location. Allow the dough to double in size (about 40 minutes to 2 hours, depending on ambient or room temperature).

11. Punch the dough down and immediately knead or press down (approximately 2 minutes) to deflate it.

12. Roll out the dough into a flat rectangle and cut it into 8-16 (or more) pieces, depending on the size desired. Make balls out of the parts.

13. Cover the balls and set them aside for 30 minutes to rest.

14 Flatten the balls and flatten them into 14-inch-thick circles using a rolling pin. Before cooking, allow the rounds to rest for approximately 5 minutes. You may also refrigerate them in a sealed jar for later use.

15. Cover uncooked rounds of dough with cloths while cooking to prevent them from drying out.

16. Brush the pitas with oil and fried them in a skillet over medium heat. Flip them over when they puff up (approximately 2 minutes on each side). Alternatively, bake them for around 2-3 minutes on greased baking pans at 350°F.

17. Can be eaten plain or with tzatziki, sliced to form a pocket, and filled with meat and/or veggies.

Chicken Gyro Pita Sandwich

Serves 2

Prep Time: 5 minutes

Time to cook: 0 minutes

Ingredients

1 recipe for chicken gyro

2 cooked gyro or pita bread

½ cup cucumber, chopped

⅓ cup yogurt

¼ teaspoon dill weed

1 clove of garlic, minced

½ small red onion, thinly sliced

1 small tomato, chopped (optional)

⅓ cup shredded lettuce (optional)

Directions

1. Combine the cucumber, yogurt, dill, and garlic in a mixing bowl. Set \saside.

2. Place part of the chicken gyro on a gyro or pita bread. Combine part of the cucumber combination, onion, tomato (optional), and lettuce in a mixing bowl (optional).

3. Serve by folding over or rolling into a wrap.rtttttt

Greek Sausage Sandwiches

Serves: 8

Time to Prepare: 10 minutes

Time to cook: 5 minutes

Ingredients

Feta sauce

1 ½ cups sour cream or Greek yogurt

1 cup feta cheese

½ teaspoon garlic powder

59

½ teaspoon oregano

Salt and pepper to taste

For sandwiches

8 pita bread

2 pounds bulk loukaniko sausage, halved lengthwise and sliced

1 long thin cucumber, diced

1 cup lettuce, shredded

4 small tomatoes, diced

2 small red onions, sliced thinly

Directions

1. Combine the sauce ingredients and put them aside to let the flavors develop.

2. Cook the sausage pieces in a pan over medium heat until they are browned. Set aside after removing from skillet.

3. Cook the onions in the pan for 1-2 minutes, or until aromatic and tender. Remove any extra fat.

4. Grill the pita to desired crispness in a nonstick pan over medium-low heat or in a sandwich press.

5. Stuff the bread with sausage, tomato, cucumber, lettuce, and caramelized onions.

6. Drizzle with roughly a spoonful of feta sauce.

Pita Sandwich with Pork Souvlaki

6 people

Time to Prepare: 10 minutes

Time to cook: 12 minutes

Ingredients

1 recipe for pork souvlaki

6 pita bread

2 cups shredded green leaf lettuce

1 small white onion, thinly sliced into half-moons

3 large round tomatoes, medium dice

½ cup olive oil

3 tablespoons red wine vinegar

1 teaspoon dried oregano

Salt and freshly ground black pepper, to taste

Tzatziki or feta sauce or crumbled feta cheese (optional)

Directions:

1. Preheat the grill to medium-high heat and grill the pork until done (remove any skewers after grilling), or fry it in a well-oiled pan over medium-high heat.

2. Toss the lettuce, onion, tomatoes, olive oil, vinegar, oregano, salt, and pepper in a medium mixing bowl.

3. Place the meat in a pita (grilled if wanted) and top with the lettuce mixture with tzatziki, feta sauce, or crumbled feta cheese (optional). Serve

Santorini Wrap - Grilled Vegetable and Feta Sandwich

Serves 3

Time to Prepare: 5 minutes

Time to cook: 8 minutes

Ingredients

3 whole pitas, warmed or toasted

For filling

3 tablespoons olive oil

1 small eggplant, cut into ½-inch by 3-inch strips

63

1 small red bell pepper, cut into ½-inch by 3-inch strips

1 small zucchini, cut into ½-inch by 3-inch strips

1 small onion, cut into ½-inch by 3-inch strips

1 clove of garlic, minced

¼ cup green olives halved

¼ cup Kalamata olives halved

¼ cup feta cheese, crumbled

3 tablespoons pepperoncini, sliced

Directions

1. Heat the olive oil in a large pan over medium heat.

2. Sauté the eggplant and zucchini strips for 4 minutes, or until soft.

3. Combine the pepper pieces, onion, and garlic in a mixing bowl.

4. Cover and simmer for 4 minutes, or until the veggies are softened.

5. Take the pan off the heat and toss in the olives, pepperoncini, and feta.

6. Cut the pita into pockets and fill them with the contents.

Kefalotyri Kefalotyri Kefalotyri Kefalotyr

12 people

Time to Prepare: 15 minutes

Time to cook: 12 minutes (on grill or skillet) or 1 hour (in the oven)

Ingredients

12 pieces of bread of choice (burger buns or pita)

4 small tomatoes, sliced

For patties

1 cup kefalotyri cheese, grated

1 pound of ground beef

1 medium onion, finely chopped

½ carrot, grated

2 sprigs parsley, finely chopped

½ teaspoon spearmint

½ teaspoon oregano

½ teaspoon paprika

½ salt or to taste

½ teaspoon pepper

1 egg, beaten

1 loaf or 10-12 slices of crustless bread, slightly soaked and strained

well

1 tablespoon olive oil

Juice of ½ an orange

Dried bread crumbs, as needed

Directions

1. In a mixing bowl, combine all of the patties' ingredients EXCEPT the kefalotyri cheese and dry bread crumbs until fully combined.

If the mixture is excessively wet or sticky, gradually add more dry breadcrumbs.

2. Preheat the oven to 375°F if baking.

3. Divide the meat mixture into 12 equal parts and shape each one into a patty.

4. Top each burger with kefalotyri.

5. Arrange the patties on a baking sheet and bake for 1 hour, or until cooked through.

6. Can also be grilled or fried in a pan over medium-high heat (about 3 minutes). Flip over until part of the flesh is slightly browned and done to your liking. Just before removing it from the fire, sprinkle with cheese.

7. Place in toast and top with tomato and tzatziki, if preferred.

BEEF/LAMB/PORK

Pork Souvlaki

serves 6

20 minutes to prepare + 3 hours to marinate.

Time to cook: 12 minutes

Ingredients

2 pounds pork shoulder, cut into 1 ¼-inch cube
68

For marinade

½ cup lemon juice

2 tablespoons red wine vinegar

2 tablespoons fresh oregano, chopped

1 tablespoon fresh thyme, chopped

1 bay leaf, finely crumbled

6 cloves garlic, minced

3 tablespoons olive oil

Salt, to taste

Freshly ground black pepper, to taste

Lemon wedges, for serving (optional)

Directions

1. Make at least six skewers. If they are made of wood, soak them in water for 1 hour before using them.

2. In a dish or resealable bag, combine the marinade ingredients (excluding the lemon wedges). Marinate the pork cubes and seal for at least 3 hours and up to overnight.

69

3. Skewer the meat and cook over medium-high heat, coating with marinade regularly, until done (about 10 minutes). Allow the final marinade application to cooking before removing it from the heat.

4. Serve with lemon wedges to squeeze over the meat before eating.

Beef kebab

4 servings

Time to Prepare: 5 minutes

Time to cook: 12 minutes

Ingredients

2 pounds beef sirloin, cut into about 1 ½-inch cube

2 bell peppers, seeded and cut into 1 ½-inch square

1 large onion cut into 1 ½-inch square

Lemon wedges

For marinade

2 tablespoons olive oil

2 tablespoons red wine vinegar

2 tablespoons lemon juice

3 cloves garlic, minced

1 tablespoon oregano

1 tablespoon dried mint

2 teaspoons kosher salt

½ teaspoon chili flakes

Directions

1. Combine the marinade ingredients in a mixing bowl. Fill a resealable bag or small pan halfway with it.

2. Place the meat on top and seal. Marinate for 30 minutes overnight, turning once or twice throughout the process.

3. Soak wooden skewers in water for an hour before using.

4. Preheat the grill to high after marinating.

5. Thread the meat and bell pepper onto the skewers alternately, taking care not to overcrowd them.

6. Grill for 8-12 minutes, coating with marinade halfway through and flipping once.

7. Allow for a 5-minute rest before serving.

Serve with lemon wedges for squeezing over the kebabs.

Burger with Beefteki and Feta

4 servings

Time to Prepare: 5 minutes

Time to cook: 16 minutes

Ingredients

1 pound lean ground beef

½ teaspoon Worcestershire sauce

1 teaspoon dried parsley

Salt and pepper to taste

1 cup crumbled feta cheese

Directions

1. Preheat the grill to medium heat and lightly grease the grate.

2. Set aside the feta cheese and properly combine the other ingredients.

3. Divide the ingredients into 8 equal-sized balls and shape them into thin patties.

4. Spread approximately 14 cups of feta cheese on four of the burgers.

5. Place another patty on top of each, pushing down on the edges to seal.

6. Cook for approximately 8 minutes on each side on a hot grill, or until well done (internal temperature of 160°F).

73

7. Serve with lemon potatoes cooked in the oven.

Lamb chops

Serves 4

Time to prepare: 5 minutes + at least 30 minutes marinating

Time to cook: 6 minutes

Ingredients

¼ cup dried oregano

2 tablespoons lemon juice

1 tablespoon garlic, minced

Salt and freshly ground pepper

8 lamb loin chops, trimmed

Directions

1. Combine the oregano, lemon juice, garlic, salt, and pepper in a mixing bowl.

Rub the spice mixture all over the lamb chops.

2. Cover, chill, and set aside for 30 minutes to 4 hours to marinate.

3. Grill or broil the lamb chops over medium-high heat for 3 minutes on each side, or until done to preference.

Moussaka

4 servings

Time to prepare: 1 hour

Time to cook: 45 minutes

Ingredients

2 medium potatoes, peeled and cut into ¼-inch circles

2-3 medium eggplants, peeled and cut into about ⅛-inch circles

Olive oil, as needed

For beef-tomato mixture

1 pound lean ground beef or lamb

1 ½ medium onions, peeled and chopped

2 tablespoons garlic, minced

1 8-ounce can of tomato sauce

1 teaspoon dried oregano

2 tablespoons dried parsley

¼ teaspoon cinnamon

¼ teaspoon nutmeg

¼ teaspoon sugar

½ teaspoon salt, or to taste

½ teaspoon fresh ground black pepper, or to taste

For white sauce

3 tablespoons butter

½ teaspoon salt

½ teaspoon fresh ground black pepper

2 tablespoons flour

1 cup half-and-half cream or milk

2 eggs, beaten

½ cup grated Parmesan cheese

Instructions for assembling the potato and eggplant layers

1. Preheat the oven to 450°F and butter a 9x13 baking dish or lasagna pan.

2. Arrange the potato slices as the first layer on the bottom of the pan. Olive oil should be brushed on.

3. Arrange the eggplant slices in a second layer on top of the potato. Brush with olive oil once more.

4. Bake for 15 minutes at 350°F.

5. Remove the eggplant and potato from the oven when they are tender. Separate a few eggplant slices to construct another layer for later.

6. Lower the heat to 350°F.

The layer of beef-tomato sauce

7. Grease a big pan and put it over medium-high heat on the stovetop.

8. Cook, tossing constantly until the meat is no longer pink and the onions are soft. Remove any extra oil or grease from the skillet.

9. Combine the garlic, tomato sauce, oregano, parsley, cinnamon, nutmeg, sugar, salt, and black pepper in a mixing bowl. Stir until well hot.

10. Spread the beef-tomato sauce mixture over the potatoes and eggplant layer in the pan.

11. Scatter the remaining eggplant pieces on top of the meat mixture.

To make the white sauce

12. Melt the butter in a skillet over medium-low heat and whisk in the flour, salt, and pepper to taste.

13. Whisk in half-and-half or milk gradually.

14. Increase the heat to medium-high and simmer, stirring constantly, until the sauce is thick and bubbling. Reduce the heat (or turn it off) when making the cheese mixture to prevent burning.

15. Place the beaten eggs in a small dish and mix in a spoonful of the hot milky sauce at a time (do not add too much hot sauce at once or the eggs will cook and solidify). Continually whisk in 4 tablespoons of the hot milky sauce. Incorporate the Parmesan cheese as well.

16. Combine the cheese sauce and the milky sauce in a mixing bowl. Cook for a few minutes more, if necessary, until the mixture thickens. Pour this over the baking dish's contents.

17. Bake for 45 minutes in a preheated oven.

18. Remove from the oven and leave aside for 15-30 minutes before slicing.

Stuffed Peppers in Greek Style

8 servings

Time to prepare: 20 minutes Time to cook: 20 minutes sautéing + 40 minutes baking

Ingredients

8 medium-sized bell peppers, any color, tops removed, seeded

1 tablespoon olive oil

½ pound ground pork

81

2 onions, chopped

Salt and pepper to taste

¼ cup dry white wine

1 10.75-ounce can of tomato puree

1 4-ounce package of feta cheese

½ cup cooked white rice

½ cup raisins

½ cup pine nuts

2 tablespoons fresh parsley, chopped

Directions

1. Preheat the oven to 350 degrees Fahrenheit.

2. Soak the bell peppers for 5 minutes in warm water.

3. In a pan over medium heat, heat the olive oil.

4. Season the pork and onions with salt and pepper and sauté until the pig is uniformly browned.

5. Transfer the sautéed pork and onion to a clean skillet, or drain the fat.

6. Simmer for 10 minutes after adding the wine and tomato puree.

Take the pan off the heat.

7. Gently fold in the feta cheese, cooked rice, raisins, pine nuts, and parsley.

Fill the peppers with the pork mixture.

9. Put the filled peppers in a baking tray and cover them with a lid or aluminum foil.

10 minutes in the oven

11. Remove the cover or foil and bake for another 10 minutes, or until the filling is gently browned (about 10 minutes)

Loukaniko - Greek Pork Sausage Made at Home

15-20 people

Time to prepare: 15 minutes + 3 hours sitting time

Time to cook: 10-15 minutes

Ingredients

5 pounds ground pork shoulder, chilled (you may use lamb or a

84

combination)

Hog casing (optional)

For seasoning

2 tablespoons garlic, finely minced

1 tablespoon dried thyme

1 tablespoon dried marjoram

1 tablespoon grated orange zest

1 tablespoon ground coriander seed

1 tablespoon dried oregano

1 tablespoon black pepper

1 tablespoon salt

1 tablespoon sugar (optional)

½ cup dry white or red wine

Directions

1. Refrigerate the ground beef until ready to use (cold meat is crucial for better binding).

2. Combine all of the seasoning ingredients and set aside for 1 hour to enable flavors to mingle.

3. Combine the spice with the cold ground pork and thoroughly mix with your hands.

4. To produce 6-inch long sausages, fill hog casings with sausage meat or use a pastry tube. You may also create patties or skinless sausages by rolling them in saran wrap.

5. Place the sausages in the freezer for at least an hour before cooking.

6. The sausage may be baked, grilled, or fried. It should be roasted until the top is practically browned.

Lamb Shanks

serve 6 people.

Preparation Time: 2 12-3 hours Cooking Time: 2 12-3 hours

Ingredients

6 lamb shanks (14-ounce pieces)

Salt, to taste

Freshly ground black pepper, to taste

Flour, for dusting

3 tablespoons olive oil

2 celery stalks, chopped

1 large onion, chopped

1 large carrot, chopped

6 large cloves of garlic, chopped

1 2-ounce can of anchovies

2 cinnamon sticks

2 small bay leaves

A handful of fresh thyme sprigs

2 tablespoons gin

¼ teaspoon ground nutmeg

1 tablespoon tomato paste

1 25-ounce bottle Merlot

2 14-ounce cans of low-salt beef broth

1 cup Kalamata olives (optional)

Directions

1. Preheat the oven to 325°F and lightly butter a baking dish.

2. Using towels, pat the lamb shanks dry. Season with salt and pepper before dusting with flour.

3. In a large ovenproof saucepan, heat the oil over medium-high heat.

4. Brown the lamb evenly in a skillet (about 10 minutes).

As you create the sauce, transfer it to a prepared baking sheet and set it in the oven to bake.

5. Stir in the following ten ingredients (celery through nutmeg).

6. Cook until the veggies begin to brown (about 20 minutes).

7. Combine the tomato paste, wine, and broth in a mixing bowl.

8. Simmer, stirring periodically, until the liquid is reduced by half (about 10 minutes).

9. Return the lamb to the sauce in a single layer in the saucepan.

Bring it to a boil.

11. Place the whole pot, including the meat, in the oven. Cook, uncovered until vegetables are soft (about 2-3 hours). Flip the shanks over and baste them as needed.

12 Remove the lamb from the pan and set it on a platter.

13. Remove any fat from the liquid and sieve the vegetable pieces into a basin, collecting the liquid.

14. Return the filtered liquid to the saucepan and bring to a boil to reduce it further, if necessary, to a gravy consistency. Season with salt and pepper to taste.

15. Return the lamb to the saucepan with the gravy and heat thoroughly.

89

16. Serve with lemon potatoes cooked in the oven.

Chicken/Poultry

Greek-Style Grilled Chicken

4 servings

Time to prepare: 10 minutes plus overnight marinating

Time to cook: 45 minutes

Ingredients

½ cup extra-virgin olive oil

1 bunch of fresh oregano, leaves picked

4 cloves garlic, finely minced

Juice of 1 lemon

Salt and freshly ground black pepper, to taste

1 whole chicken, cut into pieces

Directions

1. To marinate the chicken, pat it dry and store it in a resealable bag or shallow container.

2. Combine the other ingredients in a mixing bowl and pour over the chicken.

3. Seal the bag and flip it over several times to spread the marinade evenly over the chicken pieces.

4. Marinate overnight in the refrigerator.

5. Preheat the oven to 350°F when the marinade has finished.

6. Place the chicken skin-side down in a pan over medium-high heat.

7. Lightly brown the chicken (about 10 minutes on each side).

8. Arrange the chicken on a baking sheet and bake until golden brown (about 25 minutes).

9. Remove from the oven and set aside for 10 minutes to cool.

ten. Serve

Chicken gyro

2 servings

Time to prepare: 5 minutes + 1-hour marinating time

Time to cook: 8 minutes

Ingredients

½ pound chicken boneless breast, cut into ½-inch strips

For marinade

¼ cup lemon juice

2 tablespoons olive oil

1 clove of garlic, minced

½ teaspoon ground mustard

½ teaspoon dried oregano

Directions

1. In a resealable bag, combine the marinade ingredients.

2. Add the chicken, chill, and marinate for at least 1 hour, turning the bag over once or twice to ensure uniform flavor absorption.

3. Drain and discard the marinade when it has finished marinating.

4. Cook the chicken in a nonstick pan over medium heat for approximately 8 minutes, tossing regularly, or until done.

Chicken Baked with Rosemary and Lemon

4-6 people

Time to Prepare: 15 minutes

1 hour of cooking time

Ingredients

94

1 whole chicken (5 pounds), washed and drained

Salt and pepper

Juice of 2 lemons

For basting

2 tablespoons olive oil

½ cup butter softened

2 large sprigs of fresh rosemary, diced finely

4 cloves garlic, minced

Zest of 4 lemons

For stuffing

1 lemon, sliced

1 small onion, quartered

1 sprig rosemary

Directions

95

1. Preheat the oven to 425 degrees Fahrenheit.

2. Combine the basting ingredients in a mixing basin.

3. Dry the chicken and season it with salt and pepper; season the cavity as well.

4. Stuff the bird cavity with the sliced lemon, onion, and rosemary.

5. Brush the basting mixture over the bird.

6. Bake the chicken for 45 minutes on a baking sheet or pan.

7. Remove from the oven and baste once more with the leftover basting mixture.

8. Return to the oven and bake for 15 minutes, or until golden brown. If necessary, cover with foil to avoid burning.

9. Allow for a 15-minute cooling period before serving.

SEAFOOD

Shrimp Kebabs

2 servings

Time to Prepare: 10 minutes

Time to cook: 6 minutes

Ingredients

1 pound shrimp, shelled and deveined

Olive oil, as needed

½ teaspoon aniseed, finely crushed

Salt

Freshly-ground pepper

4 tablespoons tzatziki

¾ cup feta, crumbled

Directions

1. Preheat the grill to medium-high heat and oil the rack.

2. Thread the shrimp onto four wet wooden or metal skewers.

3. Drizzle olive oil over the shrimp and season with salt, pepper, and aniseed.

4. Grill the shrimp until they are opaque in the middle (approximately 3 minutes on each side).

5. Drizzle the tzatziki over the shrimp and top with the feta cheese.

6. Accompany with Greek salad

Grilled salmon

4 servings

Time to prepare: 20 minutes

Time to cook: 20 minutes

Ingredients

4 salmon fillets (about 1 pound)

For marinade

1 tablespoon olive oil

1 tablespoon fresh dill, chopped

1 teaspoon grated lemon peel

3 tablespoons lemon juice

2 tablespoons honey

2 cloves garlic, minced

Lemon-Dill Sauce

1 6-ounce container Greek yogurt, plain

1 tablespoon fresh dill, chopped

½ teaspoon grated lemon peel

1 tablespoon lemon juice

⅛ teaspoon pepper

Directions

1. Combine the marinade ingredients in a mixing bowl. Place aside.

2. Arrange the salmon skin-side up in a baking dish.

3. Drizzle the fish with the marinade. Cover the fillets with plastic wrap after turning them over.

4. Refrigerate the fish for 20 minutes to marinate.

5. Heat the grill to medium-high.

6. Brush the grill rack with oil and broil the salmon skin-side down.

7. Cook, covered, until the salmon flakes easily (about 10-15 minutes).

8. While the salmon is cooking, mix together the lemon-dill sauce ingredients.

9. Serve the grilled fish with the sauce.

Greek-Style Grilled Preparation

Time: 5 minutes Fish

Serves: 2

Time to cook: 25 minutes

Ingredients

1-2 entire porgy fish, trimmed and cleaned, about 12 pounds each Salt & pepper to taste

Extra-virgin olive oil from Greece

Oregano, dried

Lemon essential oil
102

1 cup olive oil from Greece

1 lemon juiced lemon wedges for serving

Directions

1. Preheat the barbeque or indoor grill to a high temperature.

2. Score both sides of the fish.

3. Brush both sides of the fish with olive oil. Season the fish on both sides and inside. On both sides of each fish, sprinkle a pinch of dried oregano.

4. To avoid adhering to the grate, place each fish in a fish grilling basket. Grill the fish for 10-20 minutes on each side, or until cooked through and the internal temperature reaches 145°F.

5. Prepare the lemon oil in the meanwhile. In a small food processor or blender, combine the olive oil and lemon juice. Blend until completely emulsified. If necessary, drizzle with olive oil. Pour into a bottle for later use.

6. When the fish is done, transfer it to a serving platter. Sprinkle some of the prepared lemon oil over the grilled porgies. Serve with lemon wedges and oregano sprinkled over top.

Squid Stuffed

4 servings

Time to Prepare: 30 minutes

1 hour of cooking time

Ingredients

8 cleaned squid, 5-6 inches each in length, cleaned and gutted,

tentacles chopped

For stuffing

2 teaspoons olive oil

1 medium onion, finely chopped

1 cup cooked rice, slightly salted

¼ cup toasted pine nuts

2 tablespoons currants, soaked in water for 10 minutes and drained

¼ cup flat-leaf parsley, finely chopped

Salt, to taste

Freshly ground black pepper to taste

For sauce

1 teaspoon olive oil

¼ cup onion, finely chopped

2 cloves garlic, minced

1 14-ounce can of tomatoes, drained and diced, juice reserved

½ cup dry white wine

1 ½ teaspoon fresh lemon juice

Salt, to taste

Freshly ground black pepper, to taste

Directions

1. Rinse and drain the cleaned and gutted squid. With towels, pat it dry.

2. Put the tentacles in a basin and leave them aside.

3. In a pan, heat the olive oil and sauté the onion for 1 minute.

4. Add the tentacles and cook for another minute. Take the pan off the heat.

5. Stir in the remaining stuffing ingredients.

6. Stuff the squid with around 2 12 teaspoons of the filling. To prevent bursting when cooking, do not overfill.

7. Use toothpicks as pins to seal the squid. Set them aside while you make the sauce.

8. Preheat a large skillet with a tight-fitting cover large enough to hold the squid in one layer.

9. Heat the oil in a skillet and sauté the onion and garlic until the onion is tender (approximately 2 minutes).

10. Stir in the other sauce ingredients and bring to a boil.

11. Arrange the stuffed squid in a single layer in the sauce.

12. Bring to a simmer, then lower to low heat and cover closely.

13. Simmer for 50–1 hour, depending on the size of the squids.

14. Check that the liquid does not dry out; if it does, add water or wine to keep it from drying out.

15. Serve immediately with some sauce.

Grilled Octopus

serves 6 people.

Time to Prepare: 15 minutes

Time to cook: 6 minutes

Ingredients

8 ounces baby octopus, cleaned

¼ cup dry white wine

2 teaspoons extra virgin olive oil

2 cloves garlic, crushed

1 teaspoon ground mild paprika

1 small fresh red chili, finely chopped

¼ cup Greek olives

Freshly ground black pepper

Salt, to taste

Lemon wedges, to serve

Directions

1. Drain the octopus after rinsing it with cool water. With towels, pat it dry.

2. Combine all of the ingredients EXCEPT the lemon wedges in a non-reactive container.

3. Add the octopus and cover it well with the spices.

4. Wrap it in plastic wrap and place it in the refrigerator for 30 minutes to marinate.

5. Preheat the grill to medium-high heat.

6. After marinating, rinse the octopus but save the marinade to make the sauce.

7. Grill the octopus for approximately 5 minutes, turning it a few times. When the octopus has been thoroughly cooked and starts to curl, it is done.

109

8. Arrange the fried octopus on a serving platter.

9. Bring the remaining marinade to a boil in a saucepan over medium-high heat. Mix in the Greek olives.

10. Season with salt and pepper and boil for 1 minute, or until slightly thickened.

11. Serve the octopus with the sauce and lemon wedges.

Vegetables and Side Dishes

Lemon Baked Potatoes

Preparation Time: 5 minutes

Servings: 2

Time to cook: 45-50 minutes

Ingredients

1 pound of potatoes, cleaned, peeled, and sliced

3 tablespoons extra-virgin olive oil

2 cloves garlic, minced

1 tablespoon Greek oregano

2 tablespoons yellow mustard

Juice of 1 lemon

¼ cup chicken or vegetable broth

Directions

1. Preheat the oven to 350 degrees Fahrenheit.

2. Combine the olive oil, garlic, oregano, mustard, and lemon juice in a mixing dish.

3. Toss in the potatoes to coat completely. Place the potatoes in a baking dish.

4. Carefully pour in the broth. Pouring over the potatoes will wash away the spices.

5. Bake the potatoes for 20-25 minutes, stirring halfway through. By this stage, the potatoes should be softening.

6. Bake for another 20-25 minutes, or until the potatoes are tender.

7. Serve with tzatziki and beefteki.

Greek-Style Grilled Vegetables in a Variety

4 servings

Time to Prepare: 10 minutes

Time to cook: 10 minutes

Ingredients

¼ cup Greek olive oil

1 tablespoon fresh lemon juice

2 cloves garlic, minced

1 teaspoon oregano

2 small eggplants, cut into 1-inch cubes

1 bell pepper, cut into 1-inch cubes

1 zucchini, cut into 1-inch cubes

1 small onion, quartered

Salt and pepper

Directions

1. In a large mixing bowl, combine the olive oil, lemon juice, garlic, and oregano.

2. Toss the sliced veggies in the oil to evenly coat.

3. Preheat the grill to medium and arrange the veggies in a single layer on the rack.

4. Brush with oil and flip once or twice. Cook until vegetables are tender.

5. Serve hot.

Spinach Lemon Spanakorizo Pilaf of rice

3-4 servings

Time to Prepare: 5 minutes

Time to cook: 15 minutes

Ingredients

2 tablespoons olive oil

1 small onion, diced

2 cloves garlic, minced

1 lemon, zested and juiced

3 cups cold cooked rice

½ cup vegetable or chicken stock

½ pound baby spinach

4 tablespoons fresh chopped dill, finely chopped

Salt and freshly ground black pepper, to taste

Crumble feta cheese and flat-leaf parsley for garnish

Directions

1. In a big deep skillet over medium heat, heat the oil.

2. Cook the onion and garlic until the onion is yellow and tender (about 2 minutes).

3. Fold in half of the dill and the young spinach. Cook for another 2-3 minutes, or until the spinach has wilted.

4. Break up any lumps in the cooked rice and combine it with the stock and lemon juice in the skillet.

5. Mix well, squeezing the rice from bottom to top to coat it with oil.

6. Turn the heat down to medium-low. Mix in the remaining dill and lemon zest. To blend, stir everything together.

7. If preferred, garnish the rice mixture with feta and parsley before serving.

If you don't have cooked rice, double the vegetable or chicken stock and add 1 cup of basmati rice to the pan. Bring the water to a boil. Cover and simmer the rice mixture for 18-20 minutes, or until the rice is tender.

Butter Beans - Gigantes Plaki Tomato Sauce Baked

4 servings

Time to prepare: 20 minutes

Time to cook: 2 hours

Ingredients

1 ½ cups dried butter beans, soaked overnight and drained

3 tablespoons extra-virgin olive oil, or as needed

1 onion, finely chopped

117

2 cloves garlic, finely chopped

2 tablespoons tomato paste

4 cups ripe tomatoes, skins removed, roughly chopped

1 teaspoon sugar

1 teaspoon dried oregano

⅛ teaspoon ground cinnamon

2 tablespoons flat-leaf parsley, chopped, plus more for garnish

Salt and pepper

Directions

1. Rinse and set the butter beans in a saucepan. Bring to a boil, covered with water.

2. Reduce the heat to low and continue to cook until the beans are cooked (approximately 50 minutes).

3. Remove the drain and put it away.

4. Preheat the oven to 350 degrees Fahrenheit.

5. Meanwhile, heat the olive oil in a large skillet or frying pan over medium heat.

6. Soften the onion and garlic in a skillet over medium heat (about 10 minutes).

7. Cook for 1 minute after adding tomato paste.

8. Stir in the other ingredients and cook for another 2-3 minutes.

9. Season with salt and pepper to taste.

10. Stir in the beans, then move to a baking dish and bake for 30 minutes.

11. Bake, uncovered until the beans are soft but not mushy (about 1 hour). While baking, do not stir.

12. Take it out of the oven and set it aside to cool.

13. Before serving, sprinkle with parsley and drizzle with olive oil.

Tzatziki - Cucumber and Yogurt Sauce

Yields roughly 2 cups

Time to Prepare: 10 minutes

Time to cook: 0 minutes.

Ingredients

½ cucumber, peeled and seeded

¼-½ teaspoon kosher salt

Zest of 1 lemon

Juice of ½ a lemon

2 cloves garlic, crushed to a paste

1 ½ cups Greek yogurt

¼ cup fresh dill

1 teaspoon ground cumin

Directions

1. Peel and grate the cucumber. It should be salted and drained in a sieve for approximately 5 minutes.

2. Squeeze or squeeze out as much water as possible from the cucumber (this is important to get a good consistency).

3. In a food processor or blender, combine all of the sauce ingredients and process until smooth.

Skordalia - Garlic and Potato Dip

3 servings

Time to Prepare: 30 minutes

Time to cook: 20 minutes

Ingredients

For boiling

122

1 pound of potatoes, scrubbed

Water for boiling

Salt

For garlic-almond paste

8 garlic cloves, minced

Salt

¾ cup whole almonds, blanched

½ cup extra virgin olive oil

½ cup water

For water-vinegar mixture

1 tablespoon + 1 teaspoon salt

5 tablespoons fresh lemon juice

3 tablespoons white wine vinegar

Fresh ground black pepper

For serving

Cut vegetables

Toasted pita triangles

Directions

1. In a saucepan, cover the potatoes with two inches of water. Bring to a boil, season liberally with salt, and serve.

2. Reduce the heat to a low setting and continue to cook until the potatoes are cooked (about 30 minutes).

3. Drain and set aside to cool somewhat.

4. Remove the skins.

5. Chop the potatoes and purée them in a food mill.

6. Using a mortar and pestle, pound the garlic. Pinch it into a paste and season with kosher salt.

7. Combine the garlic, almonds, oil, and water in a food processor. Make a paste out of it.

8. Toss the potatoes with the garlic-almond mixture. Combine thoroughly.

9. Stir in the water-vinegar mixture until well combined.

10. Season with salt and pepper to suit, and serve with sliced veggies or toasted pita bread.

DESSERT RECIPES

Galaktoboureko - Custard Pastry with Cream

15 people

Time to Prepare: 45 minutes

1 hour of cooking time

Ingredients

¾ cup butter softened

12 sheets of phyllo dough

For thickener

1 cup semolina flour

3 ½ tablespoons cornstarch

1 cup white sugar

¼ teaspoon salt

For custard

6 cups whole milk

6 eggs

½ cup white sugar

1 teaspoon vanilla extract

For syrup

1 cup water

1 cup white sugar

Directions

1. Combine the thickening ingredients in a mixing dish. To break up any lumps, sift or use a whisk or wooden spoon. Place aside.

2. Bring the milk to a low boil in a saucepan over medium heat.

3. Stir continually as you gradually add the thickening ingredients to the boiling milk.

4. Continue to whisk with a wooden spoon until the mixture thickens and bubbles.

5. Take the pan from the heat and put it aside.

6. Beat the eggs at high speed using an electric mixer.

7. Stir in the 12 cups of sugar until the mixture becomes light yellow (about 10 minutes)

8. Fold in the vanilla extract.

9. To form a custard, fold the egg mixture into the heated milk mixture. Set it aside to cool, slightly covered.

10. Preheat the oven to 350 degrees Fahrenheit.

11. Butter a 9x13 baking dish and put in 7 sheets of phyllo, coating each one with butter as you go.

12. Pour the custard over the phyllo, then top with the remaining 5 sheets of phyllo, coating each with butter as you put it down.

13. Bake until the top crust is crisp and the custard filling is set, about 30 minutes (40 to 45 minutes).

14. In a small saucepan, combine 1 cup sugar and 1 cup water to form a syrup. Bring the water to a boil.

15. Remove the Galaktoboureko from the oven and spread the hot sugar syrup over the top, paying special attention to the edges.

Allow cooling fully before slicing. Store in the refrigerator.

Baklava

serves 18 people.

Ingredients

1 16-ounce package of phyllo dough

1 pound chopped nuts

1 teaspoon ground cinnamon

1 cup butter, softened

For syrup or sauce

1 cup water

1 cup white sugar

1 teaspoon vanilla extract

½ cup honey

Directions for Cooking Time

1. Preheat the oven to 350 degrees Fahrenheit.

2. Butter the bottom and sides of a 9x13-inch baking pan.

3. Combine the chopped nuts and cinnamon in a mixing bowl and put them aside.

4. Unroll the phyllo dough stack and cut it in half to fit the pan.

5. To prevent the phyllo from drying out, cover it with a moistened cloth or towel.

6. Butter well with two sheets of dough in the pan.

7. Sprinkle the dough with 2-3 tablespoons of chopped nuts.

8. Continue with 2 sheets of phyllo, butter, and almonds until you have 6-8 layers deep.

9. Using a sharp knife, cut into diamond or square shapes all the way to the pan's bottom.

10. Bake the baklava till brown and crisp (about 50 minutes).

11. While the baklava is baking, make the syrup.

12. Combine the water and sugar in a pot and bring to a boil without stirring.

13. Once the sugar has melted, stir in the honey and vanilla extract. Cook for 20 minutes.

14. Remove the baklava from the oven and immediately drizzle with the syrup.

15. Remove it from the oven and set it aside to cool.

131

Rice Pudding Rizogalo

6 people

Time to prepare: 5 minutes + 4 hours chilling time

Time to cook: 40 minutes

Ingredients

½ cup uncooked short-grain rice

2 cups water

2 cups milk

4 tablespoons sugar

132

1 teaspoon vanilla extract

Ground cinnamon

For thickener

½ cup milk

4 tablespoons cornstarch

Directions

1. Combine the thickening ingredients in a mixing dish and put them aside.

2. Bring the rice and water to a boil in a saucepan over high heat.

3. Reduce the heat to medium-low and let it simmer, uncovered, periodically stirring.

4. Continue to cook until the water has been absorbed and the rice is tender (about 20 minutes).

5. Stir in the milk and sugar and bring to a boil over high heat.

6. Stir the thickening mixture into the rice with a quick swirl.

7. Stir in the vanilla extract. Turn off the heat in the saucepan.

8. Ladle the pudding mixture into separate serving dishes. Cool to room temperature after sprinkling with cinnamon.

9. Refrigerate for 4 hours before serving.

CONCLUSION

Cooking food at home may be inconvenient, but it is always worth it in terms of health and flavor. Some recipes are simple, while others are more complicated. Controlling the quality of the foods you use, as well as the quantity of salt or fat in the dish, provides you an advantage in your diet. If you just like cooking, creating Greek cuisine is a gratifying experience in and of itself.

Enjoy the wonderful taste and color combinations of Greek takeaway meals!

9 783986 534820